Best Easy Day Hikes
Sequoia and Kings Canyon National Parks

Help Us Keep This Guide Up to Date

Every effort has been made by the author and editors to make this guide as accurate and useful as possible. However, many things can change after a guide is published—trails are rerouted, regulations change, facilities come under new management, etc.

We would appreciate hearing from you concerning your experiences with this guide and how you feel it could be improved and kept up to date. While we may not be able to respond to all comments and suggestions, we'll take them to heart and we'll also make certain to share them with the author. Please send your comments and suggestions to the following address:

GPP
Reader Response/Editorial Department
P.O. Box 480
Guilford, CT 06437

Or you may e-mail us at:

editorial@GlobePequot.com

Thanks for your input, and happy trails!

Best Easy Day Hikes Series

Best Easy Day Hikes Sequoia and Kings Canyon National Parks

Second Edition

Laurel Scheidt

FALCON GUIDES

GUILFORD, CONNECTICUT
HELENA, MONTANA

AN IMPRINT OF ROWMAN & LITTLEFIELD

Contents

Overview Map

N

0 — Kilometers — 8
0 — Miles — 8

SEQUOIA NATIONAL FOREST

Cedar Grove Village

Road's End

180

13

14

9

10

8

Grant Grove Village and Visitor Center

The Wye

180

Big Stump Entrance

11

12

Generals Highway

20

Big Meadows Road

19

KINGS CANYON NATIONAL PARK

Stony Creek Village

KINGS CANYON NATIONAL PARK

7

Dorst Creek

6

Lodgepole Visitor Center and Village

Wuksachi Village

4

5

Wolverton

3

Crystal Cave

Crystal Cave Road

1

2

Giant Forest Museum

Crescent Meadow Road

SEQUOIA NATIONAL PARK

Ash Mountain Entrance

Foothills Visitor Center/ Park Headquarters

Silver City Resort (Private)

Atwell Mill

Mineral King Ranger Station

15

16

17

Cold Springs

198

Mineral King Road

Lookout Point Entrance

South Fork Drive

South Fork Campground

18

Hikes in the Jennie Lakes Wilderness

Introduction

Sequoia and Kings Canyon have been called "hiker's parks" because most of their area is completely roadless. Trails abound for the day hiker as well as the backpacker.

Groves of giant sequoias, waterfalls, quiet streams and meadows, wilderness lakes, and mountaintop views are all within reach of the day hiker. While some trails get heavy use, on others you may not see a soul. Every trail in Sequoia and Kings Canyon will give you something special to remember, from tiny ladybugs to immense giant sequoias, which are some of the largest living things on Earth.

The main hiking season in Sequoia and Kings Canyon is early summer through fall. Lower elevation hikes such as those in the foothills and South Fork areas are best in spring and late fall, when temperatures are comfortable and snow obstructs trails at higher elevations. Trails do tend to be more crowded on weekends and holidays and throughout the summer vacation period.

Many animals make Sequoia and Kings Canyon their home, ranging from very large in size to quite diminutive. On a day hike you will usually come across birds and squirrels, and you may even spot deer or a bear. Along with the giant sequoia, there are many other conifers in the parks. Cedars and red and white firs are just a few. Oaks and other broadleaf trees grow in the lower elevations. Hundreds of different wildflowers grow along the hillsides and in the meadows throughout the hiking season. Penstemon, wallflower, goldenrod, and shooting stars are some of the most common.

Whether you are visiting Kings Canyon and Sequoia to spot birds or wildlife, revel in the trees and the flowers, challenge your body to a physical workout, or just to find a quiet, peaceful place to clear your mind, these parks are sure to give you just what you are looking for.

Weather

The weather can turn at any time, so be prepared! Be sure to bring warm clothing and a rain poncho. A sunny day can turn into a cold and rainy one without much warning at higher elevations. Thunderstorms are common within the parks. If you become caught in a storm, take shelter. Avoid areas that are out in the open, under solitary trees, or near standing water. Stay away from metal objects that could attract lighting; crouch down and keep your feet firmly on the ground. It is also a good idea to check the weather report for the area you will be hiking in at the Sequoia National Park Web site: www.nps.gov/seki.

Wilderness Restrictions and Regulations

Some of these trails are used by horseback riders. Please remember proper trail etiquette by stepping off the trail on the downhill side and waiting quietly until the horses have passed. Stay in plain view of the horses; they may think you are a wild animal and bolt if you are hidden behind a rock or tree.

Do not shortcut trails; stay on the trail to reduce erosion and preserve vegetation. Dogs are not allowed on most trails (unless noted). Wheeled or motorized vehicles are also prohibited. If you find that you can't make it back to a restroom, bury human waste 6 inches deep, at least 100 feet from the trail, any campsites, or water sources. Do not feed any wild animals, which can make them become dependant on humans for food. Lastly, pack out all of your trash, do not pick flowers or collect souvenirs, and leave everything the way you found it.

Safety and Preparation

Bears and mountain lions live in these parks. If you happen to see one, observe it from a safe distance. If you come too close to either animal, make yourself appear as large as you can and make as much noise as possible to scare the animal away. At lower elevations, watch out for rattlesnakes, ticks, and poison oak.

Be sure to note if a trail is listed as having water available; if it doesn't, bring plenty with you. Always bring along something warm to put on if the weather changes, and wear sturdy shoes or hiking boots to reduce the risk of injury. Sunscreen, mosquito repellent, and a compass or GPS unit are also recommended. Cell phones usually cannot get service in most areas of the parks.

Visiting natural areas always imposes risks. You are responsible for your own safety. Take heed of posted warnings, be aware of your surroundings, and do not exceed your own limits. Also, leave your trip plans with a responsible party. Dial 911 for any medical emergency at park pay phones or if you can get cell phone service.

Also keep in mind that trails, facilities, and availability of restrooms and water can change at any time. It's a good idea to check with a park ranger or at a visitor center before starting your hike.

Zero Impact

Going into a wild area is like visiting a famous museum. You would not want to leave your mark on an art treasure in the museum. If everyone touring the museum left one little mark, the art would be quickly destroyed—and of what value is a big building full of trashed art? The same goes for pristine wildlands. If we all left a mark on the landscape, the backcountry would soon be spoiled.

A wilderness can accommodate human use as long as we tread on it with care. But a few thoughtless or uninformed visitors can ruin a place for everyone who follows. All backcountry users have a responsibility to know and follow the rules of zero-impact hiking.

Nowadays most wilderness users want to walk softly, but some aren't aware that the rules have changed. Often their actions are dictated by the outdated habits of a past generation of campers who cut green boughs for evening shelters, built campfires with fire rings, and dug trenches around tents. In the 1950s, these "camping rules" may have been acceptable. But such practices leave long-lasting scars, and today they are unacceptable. As the number of backcountry visitors mushrooms, wild places are becoming rare, and many camping areas show unsightly signs of heavy use.

Consequently, a new code of ethics has developed to cope with the impact of the countless masses in search of a perfect backcountry experience. Today we must leave no clue that we were there. Enjoy the wild, but strive for zero impact.

Most of us know better than to litter—in or out of the backcountry. Leave nothing, regardless of how small it is, along the trail or at a campsite. Pack out all trash, including orange peels, cigarette butts, and gum wrappers. Also pick up any trash that others have left behind.

Follow the established trail. Avoid cutting switchbacks and walking on vegetation beside the trail. Don't pick up "souvenirs," such as rocks, antlers, or wildflowers. The next person wants to see them too, and collecting such souvenirs violates many regulations.

Avoid making loud noises on the trail or at trailheads. Be courteous—sound travels easily in the backcountry, especially across water.

If possible, use restrooms or outhouses. Otherwise, carry a lightweight trowel to bury human waste 6 to 8 inches deep. Pack out used toilet paper. Keep human waste off the trail and at least 100 feet from any water source.

Finally, and perhaps most importantly, strictly follow the pack-in/pack-out rule. If you carry something into the backcountry, consume it or carry it out.

Follow these principles. Then put your ear to the ground and listen carefully. Thousands of people coming behind you are thanking you for your courtesy and good sense.

How to Use This Guide

This hiking guide is an abridged version of *Hiking Sequoia and Kings Canyon National Parks*. The guide is designed to allow readers to choose hikes best suited to their abilities and time available. Most of the hikes are 1 to 6 miles in length and gain less than 2,000 feet in elevation. All the hikes are on well-marked trails that are easy to follow; most are suitable for novice hikers and families with children.

How This Guide Is Organized

Hikes that begin in and travel through specific areas are grouped together. These areas are arranged according to the popularity of the area and the area's accessibility.

Maps

Every day hiker should carry a trail map to avoid getting lost. The National Geographic/Trails Illustrated overview map of Sequoia and Kings Canyon and inexpensive maps for Giant Forest, Lodgepole and Wolverton, Grant Grove, Cedar Grove, and Mineral King are available at the park visitor centers and online at www.sequoiahistory.org. Hikes not included on the maps mentioned above are usually covered on U.S. Geological Survey (USGS) quad maps, which are also available at visitor centers.

The U.S. Forest Service topographic trail map for the Monarch and Jennie Lakes Wildernesses is available at local map and sporting goods stores and at Forest Service offices.

Selecting a Hike

These are all easy hikes, but easy is a relative term. Hike difficulty is determined this way:

- **Easy** hikes are generally short and flat, taking no longer than an hour to complete.

- **Moderate** hikes involve increased distance and relatively mild changes in elevation, and will take one to two hours to complete.

- **More challenging** hikes feature some steep stretches, greater distances, and generally take longer than two hours to complete.

Keep in mind that what you think is easy is entirely dependent on your level of fitness and the adequacy of your gear (primarily shoes). Use the trail's length as a gauge of its relative difficulty—even if climbing is involved it won't be bad if the hike is less than 1 mile long. If you are hiking with a group, select a hike that's appropriate for the least fit and prepared in your party.

Approximate hiking times are based on the assumption that on flat ground, most walkers average 2 miles per hour. Adjust that rate by the steepness of the terrain and your level of fitness (subtract time if you're an aerobic animal and add time if you're hiking with kids), and you have a ballpark hiking duration. Be sure to add more time if you plan to picnic or take part in other activities like bird watching or photography.

Trail Finder

Best Hikes for Waterfalls

Best Hikes for Giant Sequoias

Best Hikes for Great Views

Best Hikes for Children

Best Hikes for Lakes

Best Hikes for Wildflowers

Legend

Transportation

=(180)=	State Highway
——	Park/Other Road
====	Unpaved Road

Trails

------	Featured Trail
------	Trail
→	Direction of Route

Water/Land Features

⬭	Lake
～	River/Creek
≋	Waterfall
⚲	Spring
⸚	Meadow/Marsh

Symbols

12	Trailhead
🏠	Ranger Station
■	Building/Point of Interest
P	Parking
🚻	Restroom
🔭	Scenic View
?	Visitor Center
⛰	Campground
▲	Mountain/Peak
⌣	Bridge
⌇	Pass/Gap

Land Management

▢	National Park
▢	National Forest/Wilderness

Hikes in the
Giant Forest

1   Upper Colony Mill Trail

This trek follows the old dirt road that once served as the entrance to Sequoia National Park and the Giant Forest, before the Generals Highway opened in 1926.

Distance: 5.2-mile lollipop with side trip

Approximate hiking time: 3.5 hours

Difficulty: Moderate, due to overgrown sections of trail

Trail surface: Dirt

Best season: May through early Oct

Canine compatibility: Dogs not permitted

Fees and permits: Park entrance fee; no permit required

Schedule: Gate west of the Marble Fork Bridge closes at 5:00 p.m. This gate is locked when Crystal Cave is closed for the season and may be locked at other times (refer to the signs at the turnoff).

Maps: USGS Giant Forest

Trail contacts: Sequoia and Kings Canyon National Parks, 47050 Generals Hwy., Three Rivers, CA 93271-9700; (559) 565-3341; www.nps.gov/ seki; Foothills Visitor Center, 1 mile north of the Ash Mountain entrance station

Special considerations: The parking area at this trailhead is very small; there are no restrooms or water.

Finding the trailhead: On the Generals Highway drive 13.8 miles north from the Ash Mountain entrance station, or 4.2 miles south from the General Sherman Tree area, to Crystal Cave Road. Turn onto the road and drive west for 4.1 miles, passing the Marble Fork Bridge. The small Colony Mill parking area is located on the left (south) side of the road. GPS: N36 34.15 / W118 48.25

The Hike

The old park entrance road leads west then curves south, dropping slightly through dogwoods and a shady mixed forest. Striking wild iris sometimes grows in the middle of the track. The wide path curves toward the southeast, climbing gently below Colony Peak. At the trail junction at 1.4 miles, keep left (southeast). The overgrown road to the right is your return route.

After crossing over a small ridge, the trail descends to a view above Admiration Point. Beneath you is Marble Falls, though it may not be visible through the brush growing wildly on the hillside. In the east stand the peaks of the Great Western Divide, with Moro Rock in the foreground.

The trail curves west, through chemise, manzanita, and wildflowers in spring. At 2.4 miles you arrive at the old entrance station to Sequoia National Park. The dilapidated Colony Mill Ranger Station is obviously no longer in use. The road below this point was constructed mainly with hand tools by a utopian group known as the Kaweah Colonists. They erected an infamous portable sawmill nearby in order to log the Giant Forest. In 1890 the establishment of Sequoia National Park thwarted the Colonists' plans. Thirteen years later the U.S. Cavalry extended the road (where you've been hiking) to the Giant Forest, making this the main route into the park until the Generals Highway opened in 1926.

The trail continues past toppled outhouses to the junction with your return route at 2.5 miles. Take the left (southwest) fork to the view above Panorama Point for more vistas to the east at 2.9 miles. Two abandoned trails lead off from this point: One climbs to the highest point on

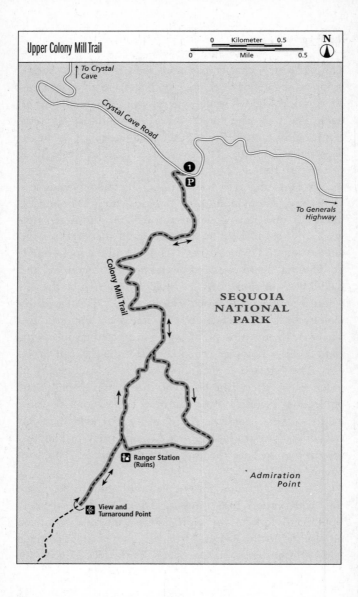

Ash Peaks Ridge, where a fire lookout was once located; the other heads downhill to the Generals Highway via Elk Creek. Both trails are now too overgrown for use. The Colony Mill Trail continues for another 7.0 miles west to North Fork Drive.

Retrace your steps to the junction with your return trail, now 3.3 miles into the hike. Keep left (north) at the fork and follow the overgrown route over the ridge. You may see mountain quail with their chicks and other wildlife in this lightly traveled area. At the junction with the main trail at 3.8 miles, turn left (north) and return to the parking area at 5.2 miles.

Option

If you want to avoid any bushwhacking, turn around at Panorama Point and return the way you came for a 5.8-mile out-and-back hike.

Miles and Directions

0.0   Start at the trailhead.

1.4   Reach the trail fork and make a left.

2.4   Arrive at the ruins of the old ranger station.

2.5   Reach the second trail fork and make a left for the side trip.

2.9   Take in the views above Panorama Point. (**Option:** Backtrack from the point for a 5.8-mile out-and-back hike.)

3.3   Return to the previous trail junction and bear left.

3.8   Reach the first trail junction; turn left and head toward the trailhead.

5.2   Arrive back at the trailhead.

2 **Crescent and Log Meadows**

This partially paved route takes you past one of John Muir's favorite meadows and to a real "log cabin." Wildlife frequents these meadows, and deer and bear sightings are common.

Distance: 1.7-mile loop
Approximate hiking time: 1 hour
Difficulty: Easy
Trail surface: Partially paved/dirt
Best season: June through Oct
Canine compatibility: Dogs not permitted
Fees and permits: Park entrance fee; no permit required
Maps: USGS Giant Forest; Sequoia National Park Giant Forest (available at park visitor centers)
Trail contacts: Sequoia and Kings Canyon National Parks, 47050 Generals Hwy., Three Rivers, CA 93271-9700; (559) 565-3341; www.nps.gov/ seki; Giant Forest Museum, 16 miles north of the Ash Mountain entrance station
Special considerations: Restrooms, water, and a picnic area are all available at this trailhead.

Finding the trailhead: On the Generals Highway, drive 15.9 miles north from the Ash Mountain entrance station, or 2.1 miles south from the General Sherman Tree area, to Crescent Meadow Road. Turn east and follow the narrow, winding road for 2.5 miles to its end at the Crescent Meadow parking area, passing the Moro Rock turnoff along the way. The trail begins at the southeast end of the parking area, just south of the restrooms. GPS: N36 33.17 / W118 44.56

The Hike

The paved path that begins this jaunt coincides with the start of the High Sierra Trail. After crossing Crescent Creek on two wooden footbridges, you take the left (east) fork, leaving the celebrated trans-Sierra route, which continues to Eagle View and then heads into the backcountry. A large sign at the end of Crescent Meadow proclaims it the "Gem of the Sierra," a quote from John Muir. Wildflowers bloom amidst the green and yellow grasses. Shooting stars and leopard lilies appear in early season, lavender lupines in the middle of summer, and bright spears of meadow goldenrods near summer's end.

The trail travels north along the southeast rim of the meadow. At 0.3 mile a dirt track leads left (north) to the Cleveland and Chimney Trees. Continue northeast on the paved path through the forest. Another dirt trail on the right loops around the east side of Log Meadow. Stay on the paved path as it takes you along the west side of Log Meadow, where, if the trail is not crowded, you may spot a bear or a doe with her young. Yellow-rumped and orange-crowned warblers often flit about in the trees above the trail.

The trail loses its pavement and reaches Tharp's Log at 0.8 mile. Hale Tharp homesteaded the Log Meadow area long before the national park was established. He may have used this dwelling—a fire-hollowed sequoia that was converted into a cabin—as a shelter while he grazed his cattle. A split-rail corral, overgrown with snowbrush, is barely visible behind a log bench.

From Tharp's Log the unpaved footpath heads north, then west, and ascends the low ridge separating the two meadows, climbing over a large log with steps carved into it. The trail descends to the Chimney Tree and the junction with the trail to the Cleveland Tree, which heads south at 1.2 miles. Proceed west around the northern tip of Crescent

Crescent and Log Meadows

SEQUOIA NATIONAL PARK

Huckleberry Trail

Chimney Tree

Tharp's Log

Crescent Meadow

Log Meadow

Crescent Creek

Crescent Meadow Road

To Generals Highway

High Sierra Trail

2

Meadow before turning left (south). The path skirts the sun-lit meadow before arriving back at the picnic area and the trailhead at 1.7 miles.

Miles and Directions

- **0.0** Start at the trailhead.
- **0.1** Continue on the paved path, staying left and passing the fork to the High Sierra Trail.

0.3 Turn right at the trail junction to the Cleveland Tree, continuing on the Tharp's Log Trail.

0.8 Arrive at Tharp's Log; then follow the trail heading left.

1.2 Reach Chimney Tree and continue straight ahead.

1.3 Pass junction with the Huckleberry Trail and turn left.

1.7 Arrive back at the trailhead.

3 Congress Trail

This paved interpretive trail takes you to the General Sherman Tree, the largest living thing on Earth, along with many other impressive "giants."

Distance: 2.7-mile lollipop
Approximate hiking time: 1.5 hours
Difficulty: Easy
Trail surface: Paved
Best season: June through Oct
Canine compatibility: Dogs not permitted
Fees and permits: Park entrance fee; no permit required
Maps: USGS Giant Forest; Sequoia National Park Giant Forest (available at park visitor centers)

Trail contacts: Sequoia and Kings Canyon National Parks, 47050 Generals Hwy., Three Rivers, CA 93271-9700; (559) 565-3341; www.nps.gov/ seki; Giant Forest Museum, 16 miles north of the Ash Mountain entrance station
Special considerations: Restrooms and water are available at the parking area. Interpretive brochures can be purchased at park visitor centers.

Finding the trailhead: On the Generals Highway, drive 1.6 miles south from Lodgepole, or 18.8 miles north from the Ash Mountain entrance station, to signed Wolverton Road. Take Wolverton Road and make a right at the road to the General Sherman Tree parking area, arriving at the trailhead in a little over 1.1 miles. The trail begins at the south end of the parking area. GPS: N36 35.5 / W118 44.58

The Hike

The trail leads downhill through the forest, crossing a horse trail from Wolverton Corrals. You will pass young sequoias on the way to the signed Congress Trail, named for some of the noteworthy trees along the trail.

After the downhill stretch, you arrive at the Leaning Tree and follow the trail over the small bridge across Sherman Creek, to the left. The trail then begins a gradual climb. The route travels through the big trees, past many numbered stops described in the interpretive pamphlet. Pass the cutoff trail at 0.7 mile and continue to the Alta Trail at 1.0 mile.

Follow the pavement to your right (west). The path leads to the left and you soon reach the fourth-largest sequoia, known as the President. The Chief Sequoyah Tree is just up the beginning of the Trail of the Sequoias, to the right (east) of the President; it is named in honor of the Cherokee Indian who developed a phonetic alphabet for his tribe.

The paved path goes on to a group of large sequoias dubbed The Senate. The footpath that leads through the center of these behemoths is the culmination of the Trail of the Sequoias. After passing a portion of Circle Meadow, the trail reaches a group of sequoias known as The House, named for the House of Representatives. After The House, you reach a five-way junction at the McKinley Tree at 1.5 miles. The trail to your left (south) leads to Circle Meadow; the Alta Trail ahead (west) leads to the site of the former Giant Forest Lodge, which has been removed to protect the giant sequoias. Turn right, heading north on the paved path.

On your left (west), a spur path leads to a photo point of the McKinley Tree, named for President William McKinley after his assassination in 1901. The trail descends, passing more interpretive stops as you approach the cutoff trail at 1.8 miles. Make your way through a tunnel in an enormous

Congress Trail

0   Kilometer   0.5
0   Mile   0.5

N

To Lodgepole

Wolverton Road

SEQUOIA
NATIONAL
PARK

Wolverton
Corrals

Generals Highway

P

3

Sherman Creek

General
Sherman Tree

Leaning
Tree

Horse Trail

Congress Trail

To
Grant Forest
Museum

Alta Trail

McKinley
Tree

The President
Chief Sequoyah
Tree

Congress
Group

Senate
Group

Trail of the Sequoias

sequoia that fell across the trail in 1965. The pathway recrosses gurgling Sherman Creek on a footbridge at 2.0 miles and heads uphill.

End this journey at the General Sherman Tree at 2.2 miles. Named for William Tecumseh Sherman, a Union general in the Civil War, this giant sequoia is the largest living organism on Earth. It is almost 275 feet tall, is about 36.5 feet in diameter at its base, and weighs approximately 1,385 tons. After taking in this awesome sight, follow the trail to the Leaning Tree and make a left to return to the parking area.

Miles and Directions

0.0 Start at the trailhead.

0.4 Reach the Leaning Tree and continue left, across the bridge.

0.7 Pass the cutoff trail and continue straight ahead.

1.0 Reach the Alta Trail and make a right.

1.1 Arrive at the junction with the Trail of the Sequoias; make a left, then a quick right to reach The Senate group.

1.5 Reach the McKinley Tree and make a right.

1.8 Pass the cutoff trail and continue straight.

2.2 Arrive at the General Sherman Tree.

2.3 Return to the Leaning Tree and make a left to retrace your steps to the parking area.

2.7 Arrive back at the trailhead.

Hikes in the Lodgepole and Dorst Areas

4 Tokopah Falls

This hike takes you to the head of glacially carved Tokopah Valley, which culminates at lovely Tokopah Falls.

Distance: 3.8 miles out and back
Approximate hiking time: 2.5 hours
Difficulty: Easy
Trail surface: Dirt
Best season: June through Oct
Canine compatibility: Dogs not permitted
Fees and permits: Park entrance fee; no permit required
Maps: USGS Triple Divide; Sequoia National Park Lodgepole and Wolverton (available at park visitor centers)

Trail contacts: Sequoia and Kings Canyon National Parks, 47050 Generals Hwy., Three Rivers, CA 93271-9700; (559) 565-3341; www.nps.gov/seki; Lodgepole Visitor Center, 21 miles north of the Ash Mountain entrance station
Special considerations: Restrooms are available at the campground and at the Lodgepole Visitor Center. Water is available at the east end of the parking area and at the visitor center.

Finding the trailhead: From the Big Stump entrance, drive east on CA 180 to the junction with the Generals Highway at 1.8 miles and make a right. Drive south a little over 25 miles, or north for about 21 miles from the Ash Mountain entrance in Sequoia National Park, to the Lodgepole turnoff and head east. Take the road into Lodgepole, past the visitor center to Lodgepole Campground. Tell the person at the gate you are going to the trailhead. Proceed to the parking area on the left (north) side of the road, before Log Bridge, and across the road from the Walter Fry Nature Center. The trail begins on the right side of the road leading to the campground, north of Log Bridge (which, although reconstructed, has retained its original name). GPS: N36 36.18 / W118 43.22

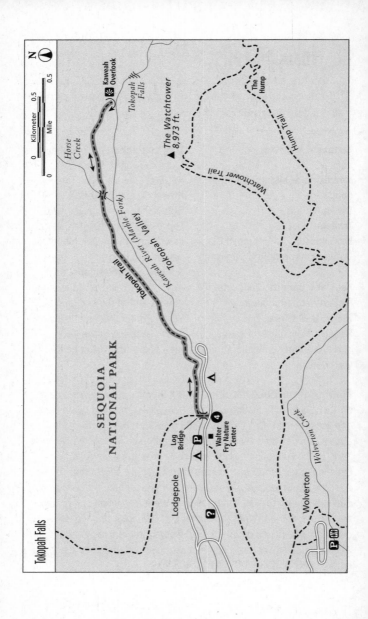

The Hike

The trail begins by following the north bank of the Marble Fork of the Kaweah River. A trailbed has been chiseled into a section of granite here. Be careful as you traverse the smooth, sometimes slippery rock.

As you enter the forest you may notice colorful tents and sounds of civilization in the campground across the river. Those reverberations soon fade away. Spur trails lead down to the river throughout this hike; be sure to keep to the left at these junctions, and keep to the right on the return trip. If you decide to explore these spur trails, exercise extreme caution near swift-moving areas of the river and during peak runoff periods in early summer.

Tokopah Valley was shaped by a glacier, much like Yosemite Valley and the Cedar Grove area of Kings Canyon. A view of the Watchtower, the large, pointed granite monolith on the south wall of the valley, opens up to your right (southeast). This crag was too solid to be ground down by the ice sheet, and it seems to change shape as you travel on toward the falls. While continuing through firs and lodgepole pines, you pass small meadows where you may see a deer or bear.

The trail leads up and over a couple of small ledges before reaching the first branch of Horse Creek at 1.4 miles. Three footbridges help you cross the many-forked creek. The trail then cuts across a wash, which usually contains water only in early spring and can be crossed on stones if water is present.

As you leave the forest, you gain a view of Tokopah Falls in its entirety. The trail then winds through willows and boulders; it is edged with brilliant red penstemons in summer. As you near the falls overlook, you may see marmots and even a pika among the talus blocks and boulders. The overlook is at 1.9 miles. A sign warns visitors not to continue up the canyon to the falls due to injuries and deaths that have occurred here in the past.

After enjoying a safe view of the falls, return the way you came to reach the trailhead at 3.8 miles.

Miles and Directions

0.0 Start at the trailhead.

1.4 Begin crossing several branches of Horse Creek.

1.9 Reach the Tokopah Falls overlook and take in the view. When ready, retrace your steps.

3.8 Arrive back at the trailhead.

5 Heather Lake

This jaunt culminates at the first lake on the Lakes Trail. Heather Lake is a tranquil pool of water, its shores lined with red heather.

Distance: 8.2 miles out and back
Approximate hiking time: 5 hours
Difficulty: Moderate, due to length and elevation gain
Trail surface: Dirt
Best season: Mid-June through Oct
Canine compatibility: Dogs not permitted
Fees and permits: Park entrance fee; no permit required
Maps: USGS Lodgepole; Sequoia National Park Lodgepole and Wolverton (available at park visitor centers)
Trail contacts: Sequoia and Kings Canyon National Parks, 47050 Generals Hwy., Three Rivers, CA 93271-9700; (559) 565-3341; www.nps.gov/seki; Lodgepole Visitor Center, 21 miles north of the Ash Mountain entrance station
Special considerations: Restrooms and water are available at the south side of the parking area.

Finding the trailhead: Drive 1.6 miles south from Lodgepole on the Generals Highway, or 0.5 mile north from the General Sherman Tree parking area, to signed Wolverton Road. Turn east and follow Wolverton Road for 1.5 miles to the parking area at its end. The trail begins on the north side of the parking area. GPS: N36 35.48 / W118 44.3

The Hike

Begin by climbing up some concrete steps and head north on the signed Lakes Trail. On your way uphill, you meet

Heather Lake

SEQUOIA NATIONAL PARK

Lodgepole

To Dorst Campground

Generals Highway

Log Bridge

Walter Fry Nature Center

Tokopah Trail

Kaweah River (Marble Fork)

Tokopah Valley

Tokopah Falls

Kaweah Overlook

The Watchtower 8,973 ft.

Watchtower Trail

To Emerald Lake

Heather Lake

The Hump

Hump Trail

Panther Gap Trail

Lakes Trail

Wolverton

Wolverton Creek

Long Meadow Trail

Wolverton Road

To Giant Forest

N

0   1   Kilometer

0   1   Mile

an unsigned trail to your left (west); this is part of the Long Meadow Trail. Continue around the curve to a junction at 0.1 mile with a connector trail leading to Lodgepole and the Sherman Tree Trail. Keep right (east). Almost immediately, you will pass another junction with the Long Meadow Trail.

Your path travels up a moraine deposited by the Tokopah Glacier millions of years ago. The trail nears the tinkling sounds of Wolverton Creek, and a lush meadow appears on the right (south).

The trail curves to the southeast, travels through clearings in the dense woodland, and crosses a creeklet. At the junction with the Panther Gap Trail at 1.7 miles, turn left (northeast). The path recrosses the same small watercourse and meets the Hump Trail at 2.0 miles. Keep left (northeast) on the Watchtower Trail, which is less steep and has better views from its cliffside route.

The trail climbs to a meadow, where you can cross its creek easily on stones. The grade steepens; you may see a marmot or hear one of its loud chirps as you climb. Moments later the trail switchbacks and deposits you next to the Watchtower, the colossal granite spire on the south side of Tokopah Valley.

After examining the Watchtower and Tokopah Falls, 1,500 feet below, continue east on a shelf blasted out of the rock. Views up and down the valley seem endless. The trail is wide and easy to follow as it climbs, then descends, to meet the other end of the Hump Trail. Enter a thinly forested area. At 4.1 miles you reach Heather Lake, named for the red heather lining its shores. A short trail to the north leads to an open-air pit toilet (toilet paper is not supplied).

After taking in the peacefulness of Heather Lake, backtrack to the parking area at 8.2 miles.

Miles and Directions

0.0   Start at the trailhead and climb the concrete steps.

0.1   Reach the junction with the Wolverton Trail and make a right.

1.7   Meet the Panther Gap Trail junction and make a left to stay on the Lakes Trail.

2.0   Arrive at the Watchtower/Hump Trail junction and continue straight ahead.

4.1   Reach tranquil Heather Lake. When ready, retrace your steps.

8.2   Arrive back at the trailhead.

6 Little Baldy

The summit of Little Baldy gives a spectacular view of the Silliman Crest, the Kaweah Peaks, and the lower portion of the Great Western Divide.

Distance: 3.4 miles out and back
Approximate hiking time: 3 hours
Difficulty: Moderate, due to elevation gain
Trail surface: Dirt
Best months: June through Oct
Canine compatibility: Dogs not permitted
Fees and permits: Park entrance fee; no permit required
Maps: USGS Giant Forest
Trail contacts: Sequoia and Kings Canyon National Parks, 47050 Generals Hwy., Three Rivers, CA 93271-9700; (559) 565-3341; www.nps.gov/seki; Lodgepole Visitor Center, 21 miles north of the Ash Mountain entrance station
Special considerations: Restrooms and water are not available at this trailhead. During storms, there is a risk of being struck by lightning on the summit of Little Baldy. If you see dark clouds nearby, hear thunder, or observe hail, rain, or static electricity in the air, descend immediately.

Finding the trailhead: Drive 6.6 miles north from Lodgepole on the Generals Highway, or 1.5 miles south from Dorst Campground, to the signed Little Baldy Saddle. Parking is available on both sides of the road. The trail begins on the east side of the road, marked by a large sign. GPS: N36 37.12 / W118 48.33

The Hike

The trail begins by climbing a few stone steps and a short switchback (not shown on some maps). At 0.1 mile, the end of this switchback, you may discern an old, abandoned trailbed that leads back to the road. Continue uphill on a long traverse through a thick forest of tall pine and fir trees. As you near the next switchback at 0.4 mile, a view opens up to the west, revealing Big Baldy and Chimney Rock. Many wildflowers grow here in summer. You may even see marmots among the large boulders above the path.

Continuing on this open, sometimes rocky portion of the trail, you meet two more switchbacks before the trail levels off. At 1.0 mile a very quiet wooded area is a good place to stop and listen to the silence.

After leaving this peaceful place and rounding a hilltop at 1.3 miles, you begin to have views to the east of the Kaweahs and the Great Western Divide. The trail brings you through intermittent forest to the base of Little Baldy's granite dome, contours around the south side, and leads on to the summit at 1.7 miles.

Spanish Mountain and Obelisk are visible to the north. To the east are Mount Silliman, Alta Peak, the Kaweah group, and the Great Western Divide extending south to Farewell Gap. In the foreground to the south-southeast, you can see the tip of Moro Rock and the Castle Rocks. On a clear day look west; you may even be able to see the San Joaquin Valley, a backdrop to Big Baldy Ridge and Chimney Rock.

After enjoying the view, retrace your steps to the trailhead at approximately 3.4 miles.

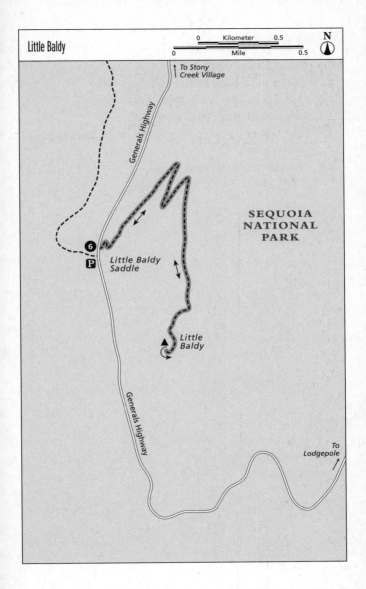

Miles and Directions

0.0 Start at the trailhead.

0.4 Enjoy the view of Big Baldy and Chimney Rock.

1.0 Enter a quiet wooded area as the trail levels out.

1.3 Look out toward the Great Western Divide.

1.7 Attain the summit of Little Baldy. When ready, head back the way you came.

3.4 Arrive back at the trailhead.

7 Muir Grove

This hike takes you to a less frequently visited sequoia grove, with views of Big Baldy and Chimney Rock along the way.

Distance: 4.0 miles out and back
Approximate hiking time: 3.5 hours
Difficulty: Moderate, due to slippery areas on trail
Trail surface: Dirt
Best season: June through Oct
Canine compatibility: Dogs not permitted
Fees and permits: Park entrance fee; no permit required
Maps: USGS Muir Grove
Trail contacts: Sequoia and Kings Canyon National Parks,
47050 Generals Hwy., Three Rivers, CA 93271-9700; (559) 565-3341; www.nps.gov/seki; Lodgepole Visitor Center, 21 miles north of the Ash Mountain entrance station
Special considerations: When the campground is open, late June through Labor Day, parking, restrooms and water are available. Otherwise, park at the gate on the Generals Hwy. with an additional 1.6 miles added to the hike.

Finding the trailhead: Follow the Generals Highway 5 miles south of Stony Creek Village, or 8.2 miles north of Lodgepole, to the Dorst Campground entrance. Drive west into the campground. Follow the signs to the amphitheater and a parking area at 0.9 mile, just beyond the group campground entrance. The signed trail begins on the left side of the road leading into the group campground, across from campsite 'E'. GPS: N36 38.1/W118 48.59

The Hike

The trail leads into the forest and makes a right at the junction with the trail from the former trailhead. Descend a

Muir Grove

N

0   Kilometer   0.5

0   Mile   0.5

To Stony
Creek Village

Generals Highway

Lost Grove Trail

Dorst
Campground

Dorst Creek

P

7

Dome

SEQUOIA
NATIONAL PARK

MUIR GROVE

switchback and meet a north-trending trail to Dorst Creek at 0.1 mile. Follow the fork to the left (west), the signed Muir Trail; a fern-filled meadow is on your right. The trail travels through a thick fir forest, where you may hear the peaceful song of the hermit thrush.

Pass over granite slabs, and step across another tributary at 0.6 mile before coming to a fork. What appears to be a climber's trail departs from the base of a couple of long switchbacks; this side trail continues straight toward the base of the granite dome above and is feebly blocked by some branches. Turn left (south), traveling uphill. At 1.0 mile you arrive at a path leading to the high point of this dome, with a view of Big Baldy and the east face of Chimney Rock. You can also see the sequoias of Muir Grove, this hike's destination, on the ridge west of here.

The trail passes into the trees again and then enters a rocky area, traversing a steep portion of loose rock. Watch your step. After reentering the forest, the trail comes to another tributary at 1.6 miles. Those with good balance can cross on a large fallen tree. If you prefer a lower crossing, you will find some stones to aid your passage a few steps past the tree. Now the path narrows and becomes slightly over-grown, but it remains easy to follow. Continue up the steep hillside until you reach a gigantic sequoia at the entrance to Muir Grove at 2.0 miles.

There are myriad paths to explore. A short track to the left ends abruptly in a group of giant sequoias. The path to your right travels uphill, splits, rejoins, and leads to a sequoia hollowed out by fire; it ends at a lupine-covered hillside. Another footpath proceeds straight ahead into a group of sequoias, fizzling out just past them. The route heading downhill to the southwest is the last remnant of the main trail. The path used to continue to Skagway Grove, Hidden Spring, and Crystal Cave. That section of the trail has not been maintained in more than forty years. The route now ends about 50 feet from an immense sequoia that fell across the trail, guaranteeing its return to a natural state.

After you have explored the grove, return the way you came to reach the trailhead at 4.0 miles.

Miles and Directions

0.0 Start at the trailhead.

0.1 Reach the trail fork with the Lost Grove Trail and make a left.

0.6 Cross the first unnamed creek.

1.0 Reach a side trail to the dome overlook.

1.6 Cross the second unnamed creek.

2.0 Enter Muir Grove and explore. When finished, return the way you came.

4.0 Arrive back at the trailhead.

Hikes in the
Grant Grove Area

8 Big Stump Loop

This interpretive trail takes you through an area that was heavily logged in the 1880s. The stumps and fallen trees now serve as a reminder of how important it is to protect our environment. Although General Grant National Park was established in 1890 and incorporated in Kings Canyon National Park in 1940, Big Stump Basin was not included until 1965.

Distance: 2.0-mile loop
Approximate hiking time: 1 hour
Difficulty: Easy
Trail surface: Dirt
Best season: May through Oct
Canine compatibility: Dogs not permitted
Fees and permits: Park entrance fee; no permit required.Maps: USGS General Grant Grove; Kings Canyon National Park Grant Grove (available at park visitor centers)
Trail contacts: Sequoia and Kings Canyon National Parks,
47050 Generals Hwy., Three Rivers, CA 93271-9700; (559) 565-3341; www.nps.gov/seki; Grant Grove Visitor Center, 3 miles east of the Big Stump entrance station
Special considerations: Restrooms, water, picnic tables, and barbecues are available at the parking area. You may purchase an interpretive booklet for this trail from a coin-operated machine at the trailhead and also at park visitor centers.

Finding the trailhead: From the park boundary on CA 180, drive 0.9 mile to the Big Stump entrance station, on the left (west) side of the road. The trail begins on the south side of the parking area, near the restrooms. GPS: N36 43.15 / W118 58.14

The Hike

As you head downhill (southeast), you almost immediately come to the Resurrection Tree. This giant's top was destroyed by lightning, and it is now "resurrecting" a new one. Beyond lies the Shake Pile, a toppled sequoia that was chiseled apart to make fence posts, roof shingles, and grape stakes. Though extremely rot and fire resistant, sequoia wood is very brittle; because of the immense size of these trees, they often shattered when felled.

At 0.3 mile the trail forks. Take the route to the left (east). It leads to the Burnt Monarch, known to the loggers as Old Adam. This huge, burned-out sequoia was used to store snow, allowing for ice in the summer months when the logging mill was in operation.

The trail continues to two sequoias planted in 1888. They have reached great heights in their hundred-plus years, but not the girths of the old "giants." An abandoned road grade joins the trail just beyond these trees. Farther down the trail, a meadow serves as the site of the Smith–Comstock Mill. All that remains are the wood posts of the foundation sticking up through the grass to your right (west). Notice the piles of reddish-brown sawdust that still remain more than one hundred years later.

A bit farther down the path is a side trail to the Featherbed. This trench was dug and lined with branches from other felled trees to cushion the fall of one of the "Big Trees." Observant hikers may spot other featherbeds in the area. At 0.6 mile the trail forks again. Turn right (west), traveling around the little meadow to the Shattered Giant. This tree smashed into so many pieces that it was practically

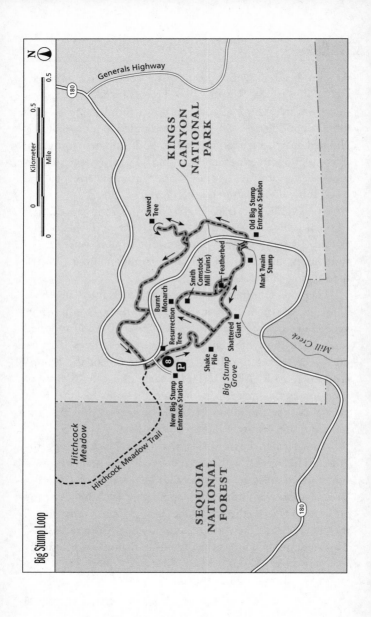

Big Stump Loop

unsalvageable. Now it serves as a bridge over the tiny tributary that flows through the meadow.

Retrace your steps around the meadow to the previous junction and turn right (east). Pass another portion of the Featherbed loop and cross Mill Creek on a wooden bridge. On the other side is the Mark Twain Stump. This sequoia was felled in 1891 so that the American Museum of Natural History in New York could exhibit a slice. Steps lead to the top of the stump, and standing in the center gives you an even better idea of how large these trees really are. Also visible are the healed burn scars from fires the tree survived.

From the Mark Twain Stump the trail makes a short climb to CA 180 at 1.0 mile. Follow the crosswalk and continue uphill on the other side. Traveling through the forest, you reach the side trail to the Sawed Tree at 1.3 miles. Turn right (northeast) and take the path up a few short switchbacks to this survivor. When loggers realized the tree could not be felled in the direction they wanted, they moved on. The Sawed Tree still continues to heal.

To return to the main trail, retrace your steps. At the last switchback, an abandoned section of trail to the left (south) is passable until just before it reaches the main trail, where it is blocked by thorny ceanothus, or snowbrush. (If you venture off here, retrace your steps.) Upon returning to the main trail, stay right (northwest) and pass through more forest and manzanita clearings to a short downhill. The path then follows a long, thin meadow to a large culvert that allows you to pass under CA 180 and meet the start of the Hitchcock Meadow Trail. Turn left (south) and climb to the parking area at 2.0 miles.

Miles and Directions

0.0   Start at the trailhead.

0.3   Reach the first trail fork and go left.

0.6   Reach the second trail fork and make a right.

1.0   The trail crosses CA 180 after passing the Mark Twain Stump.

1.3   Take the side trail leading to the Sawed Tree, then return to the main trail and make a right.

2.0   Arrive back at the trailhead.

⑨ General Grant Loop

This paved interpretive trail takes you through the heart of the General Grant Grove to the General Grant Tree. Named for Ulysses S. Grant, this tree has been declared the nation's Christmas tree and a living national shrine honoring Americans who died in war. The trail also passes the historic Gamlin Cabin.

Distance: 0.8-mile loop
Approximate hiking time: 45 minutes
Difficulty: Easy
Trail surface: Paved
Best season: May through Oct
Canine compatibility: Dogs not permitted
Fees and permits: Park entrance fee; no permit required
Maps: USGS General Grant Grove; Kings Canyon National Park Grant Grove (available at park visitor centers)
Trail contacts: Sequoia and Kings Canyon National Parks, 47050 Generals Hwy., Three Rivers, CA 93271-9700; (559) 565-3341; www.nps.gov/seki; Grant Grove Visitor Center, 3 miles east of the Big Stump entrance station
Special considerations: Restrooms and water are available at this large parking area. You may purchase an interpretive pamphlet for this trail from the coin-operated machine at the trailhead or at the Grant Grove Visitor Center.

Finding the trailhead: From the Big Stump entrance station, drive north on CA 180, past Grant Grove Village, to the junction with the road leading to the Grant Tree. Turn left (west) and drive to the Grant Tree parking area, which is 3.5 miles from the entrance station. The paved trail begins at the large sign on the north side of the parking area. GPS: N36 44.50 / W118 58.25

The Hike

Begin this paved loop by taking the right fork to the Robert E. Lee Tree, the thirteenth-largest tree in the world. Many sequoia groves were explored around the time of the Civil War, and some of the trees were given names of those made famous by that conflict. The General Grant Tree is farther along the route. First proceed just past the east end of the tree known as the Fallen Monarch to Photo Point. From this alcove you can take a picture of the entire Grant Tree from base to crown. Continuing on, you reach young sequoias that were planted around 1949. The trees contrast in size because of the different amounts of water and light each receives.

While giant sequoias are the main attraction, they are not the only trees in the grove. A sign describes the other trees, including white fir, incense cedar, sugar pine, and ponderosa pine. The Tennessee Tree, a giant sequoia, and Pacific dogwood trees are just ahead. If you are here in June, the dogwoods may be covered with soft, white blossoms.

Next you arrive at this trail's namesake, the General Grant Tree. This tree is the world's third-largest living organism. It has a greater base diameter than any other sequoia. An unpaved trail circles the General Grant Tree and meets a side trail that leads you to the Vermont Log (which fell in 1985).

On the main trail, continue on to the Gamlin Cabin. Built by the Gamlin brothers in 1872, this historic cabin served as the first ranger station for General Grant National Park, which was included in Kings Canyon National Park in 1940. Parts of the cabin have been restored, and a concrete foundation has been added to preserve the structure.

If you wish to visit North Grant View, another good photo opportunity, take the trail to the right (east) of Gamlin Cabin and proceed a few hundred feet uphill to the North Boundary Trail. Turn left (west) at the junction, walk in a short distance, and look back (southeast) toward the Grant Tree. The top-to-bottom view provides a different perspective from that at Photo Point.

Beyond the Gamlin Cabin you will find the Fire-Damaged Trees, which illustrate the fire resistance of sequoias, and the Centennial Stump. This stump is all that remains of a sequoia felled in 1875 so that a 16-foot section could be taken to the Centennial Exhibition in Philadelphia the following year. The tree was cut into segments for transportation and reassembled at the exhibition. Spectators thought it was many trees put together to resemble a single big tree and dubbed it the "California Hoax." Later the stump was known as the "School Stump," as Sunday school classes were held on it during the logging era.

The route continues to the California Tree, which was struck by lightning in 1967. A park forester climbed this tree with a fire hose and put out the blaze to preserve the sequoia grove. The Oregon Tree View is just down the trail and to the right (northwest). The route has now looped to the west end of the Fallen Monarch. This huge tree sheltered the Gamlin brothers and others. It has been used as a hotel and saloon, and the U.S. Cavalry stabled their horses here while patrolling General Grant National Park.

As you near the end of the loop you reach the Lincoln Tree and a view of the Twin Sisters, two sequoias that have fused together on the west side of the parking area. When you have reached the parking area, you will notice the

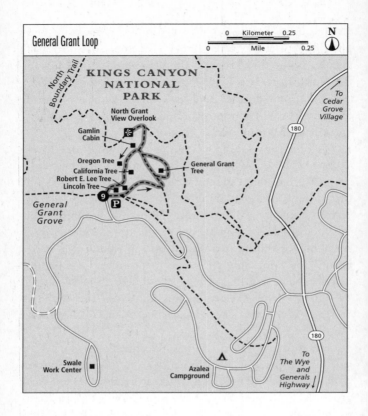

group of mature sequoias to your left, known as the Happy Family. These trees are about the same age and probably sprouted after a very intense fire cleared the spot where they have grown. The loop ends at 0.8 mile.

10 North Grove and Dead Giant Loops

This hike takes you through the northern portion of the General Grant Grove, past an old logging camp road and to the overlook of a beautiful lake.

Distance: 2.5-mile double loop
Approximate hiking time: 2 hours
Difficulty: Easy
Trail surface: Dirt
Best season: May through Oct
Canine compatibility: Dogs not permitted
Fees and permits: Park entrance fee; no permit required
Maps: USGS Hume and General Grant Grove; Kings Canyon National Park Grant Grove
(available at park visitor centers)
Trail contacts: Sequoia and Kings Canyon National Parks, 47050 Generals Hwy., Three Rivers, CA 93271-9700; (559) 565-3341; www.nps.gov/seki; Grant Grove Visitor Center, 3 miles east of the Big Stump entrance station
Special considerations: Restrooms and water are available at this large parking area.

Finding the trailhead: From the Big Stump entrance station, drive north on CA 180, past Grant Grove Village, to the junction with the road leading to the Grant Tree. Turn left (west) and drive to the Grant Tree parking area, which is 3.5 miles from the entrance station. The trail begins at the westernmost lower parking area (reserved for RVs and trailers) at the gate signed NORTH GROVE LOOP. GPS: N36 44.50 / W118 50.30

The Hike

The trail begins by following a closed road, which is also part of the Sunset Trail. Hike downhill through the dappled

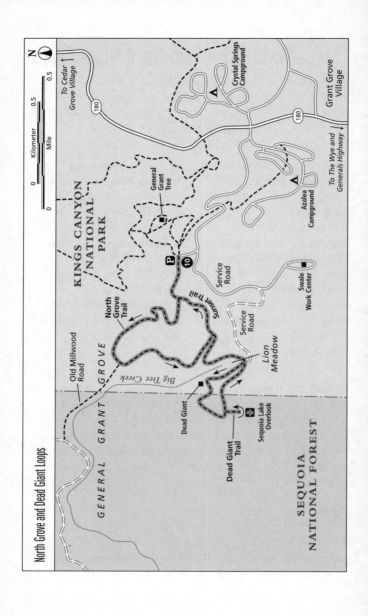

North Grove and Dead Giant Loops

light of the shady forest. At 0.1 mile you reach the North Grove Trail junction. Turn right (northwest) on the North Grove Trail. The wide path winds between numerous sequoias while continuing to descend. At 0.6 mile you arrive at the unsigned junction with the Old Millwood Road, which resembles a small gully leading into the brush to your right (northwest). If you step through the overgrowth, you will see the gully widen to a one-lane dirt road. The Old Millwood Road leads 2.3 miles (with an elevation loss of 920 feet) to the site of Millwood, an old logging camp.

Beyond the junction, the trail climbs past an immense burned sequoia and more of the "giants" before returning to the closed road. At 1.1 miles you will reach the junction with the Sunset Trail. Turn right (south) and follow the road around pretty Lion Meadow. At 1.3 miles you reach the junction with the Dead Giant Trail. Turn right (northwest) on the first, and lower, of two parallel paths. (You will return via the other trail.) The path travels above the edge of the deep green meadow and brings you to the Dead Giant, a large girdled sequoia that still stands.

The trail turns to the southwest and climbs uphill past a trail sign to the top of the ridge, through clearings in the manzanita. As the wide track levels, another trail sign indicates a left turn. Continue straight ahead to the Sequoia Lake overlook at 1.7 miles. Framed by cedars and pines, this sapphire-blue lake is man made. The Sanger Lumber Company dammed Sequoia Creek in 1889 to supply water for the flume that supported logging operations in the area. The flume stretched 54 miles to the town of Sanger and cost $300,000 to construct.

After viewing the lake, return to the previous trail sign and turn right (east). Follow the trail downhill, back into the forest. At 1.9 miles you meet the closed road. Turn left (north) onto the road, following it past the two junctions with the North Grove Trail and back to the trailhead at 2.5 miles.

Miles and Directions

0.0 Start at the trailhead.

0.1 Reach the North Grove Trail junction and make a right.

0.6 Pass the Old Millwood Road junction.

1.1 Meet the first Sunset Trail junction and make a right.

1.3 Meet the Dead Giant Trail junction and make another right.

1.7 Make a right at the side trail to Sequoia Lake overlook, then retrace your steps to the main trail and turn right again.

1.9 Reach the second Sunset Trail junction and make a left.

2.5 Arrive back at the trailhead.

Hikes around
Redwood Mountain

11 Hart Tree Loop

This jaunt takes you to an old logging camp, a sequoia "log cabin," a pretty meadow, and a waterfall, all while traveling through the largest sequoia grove left standing on the planet.

Distance: 7.2-mile loop
Approximate hiking time: 4.5 hours
Difficulty: Moderate, due to length
Trail surface: Dirt
Best season: May through June; Oct through Nov
Canine compatibility: Dogs not permitted
Fees and permits: Park entrance fee; no permit required

Maps: USGS General Grant Grove
Trail contacts: Sequoia and Kings Canyon National Parks, 47050 Generals Hwy., Three Rivers, CA 93271-9700; (559) 565-3341; www.nps.gov/seki; Grant Grove Visitor Center, 3 miles east of the Big Stump entrance station
Special considerations: An out-house is located at this trailhead, but no water is available.

Finding the trailhead: From the Big Stump entrance, drive east on CA 180 to the junction with the Generals Highway at 1.2 miles and make a right. Drive south 3.5 miles to Quail Flat. Turn right (south) onto the dirt road across from the paved road leading to Hume Lake. Drive approximately 2 miles to a junction at a large, modern cabin. Take the left (southeast) fork, which leads through a fallen sequoia and continues for another 0.2 mile to the parking area. The trail begins at the southwest end of the parking area, to the left of the bulletin board, and is signed HART TREE and REDWOOD CANYON. GPS: N36 42.28 / W118 55.15

The Hike

The wide trail (once a dirt road) heads downhill (south), past a fire hydrant and through mixed firs, pines, and giant sequoias. A view of Buena Vista Peak appears as the path rounds a turn and switchbacks. The junction with the Redwood Canyon Trail is at 0.3 mile. Turn left (north) onto the Hart Tree Trail; the other path will be your return route.

Wild strawberries carpet the forest floor as you proceed. After stepping across fledgling Redwood Creek, you arrive at Barton's Post Camp at 0.5 mile. Large sequoia stumps and a few felled trees are the only evidence of the small-scale logging operation that manufactured fence posts here in the late 1800s.

The path crosses a small ridge and dips across an unnamed brook before reaching the deteriorating Pierce Cabin at 0.8 mile. This fire-hollowed sequoia had shingles, fireplaces, and a door added to make it habitable at one time; today it is sadly collapsing. Climb onto to a granite-and-manzanita-covered knob at 0.9 mile. A few steps off the trail will give you an excellent view to the west of the crowns of sequoias growing on Redwood Mountain.

After the viewpoint, descend to cross another unnamed creeklet at 1.0 mile. The trail rises again, ascending a switchback, then travels through oaks. Beyond another easily spanned rivulet, climb to a rocky knoll at 1.7 miles. Look west for views of Redwood Mountain and south toward Big Baldy Ridge and the Redwood Canyon.

The trail then drops down through wild roses to lovely Hart Meadow, with Buena Vista Peak as the backdrop. At 1.9 miles you advance gingerly through a muddy area at the lower end of the meadow. Here the trail crosses a couple of branches of Buena Vista Creek, which are lined with white mountain violets and sword ferns.

The route mounts the next ridge and then passes through the entire length of a fire-hollowed sequoia. (A bypass is available for the claustrophobic.) You wind your way down through fallen "giants" to the East Fork of Redwood Creek at 3.0 miles. This creek crossing can be a little tricky in early season if you are not wearing waterproof boots.

The trail ascends to a steep spur path at 3.2 miles, flanked by two signs and leading to the Hart Tree. At one time this behemoth was ranked as the fourth-largest sequoia in the world, but other trees have surpassed it. The route then descends to a pretty, unnamed creek with a peaceful water-fall and an easy crossing on stones at 3.5 miles. A muddy seep intersects the path on the other side of this creek.

Begin the long decline to the bottom of the canyon, crossing one more tiny brook at 3.9 miles. Along the way you may spot tiny winter wrens darting around the many sequoia trunks near grassy areas.

After passing through large zones of wild rose and bear clover, you reach the immense Fallen Goliath at 4.7 miles. The path descends to Redwood Creek and a campsite to the right (north) at 5.2 miles. This crossing can be tricky without waterproof boots in early season, but the creek is easily crossed on stones in the fall. Alders and dogwoods line the creek, the latter decorated with delicate white blooms in June. Autumn brings an exhilarating color show, as the deciduous trees turn beautiful hues of light green, gold, and red.

On the other side of the creek, you come to a junction with the Redwood Canyon Trail; turn right (northwest). At 5.3 miles you pass the junction with the Sugarbowl Trail

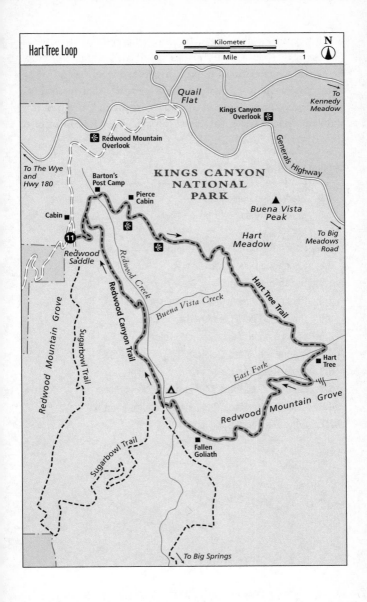

Hart Tree Loop

0 — Kilometer — 1
0 — Mile — 1

N

Quail Flat

Kings Canyon Overlook

Redwood Mountain Overlook

To Kennedy Meadow

KINGS CANYON NATIONAL PARK

To The Wye and Hwy 180

Barton's Post Camp

Pierce Cabin

Cabin

11

Redwood Saddle

Buena Vista Peak

Hart Meadow

To Big Meadows Road

Redwood Creek

Redwood Mountain Grove

Sugarbowl Trail

Redwood Canyon Trail

Buena Vista Creek

Hart Tree Trail

East Fork

Hart Tree

Redwood Mountain Grove

Sugarbowl Trail

Fallen Goliath

To Big Springs

Generals Highway

as your path climbs gradually along meandering Redwood Creek. The route switchbacks as it moves up the slope from the watercourse, continuing past many "Big Trees" and working its way around three sequoias that have fallen across the old roadbed. At 6.9 miles, you reach the junction with the Hart Tree Trail. Turn left and retrace your steps to the parking area at 7.2 miles.

Miles and Directions

0.0 Start at the trailhead.

0.3 Meet the Redwood Canyon Trail junction and take the trail to the left.

0.5 Reach the Barton's Post Camp.

0.8 Reach the Pierce Cabin.

1.7 Reach a viewpoint.

1.9 Cross the branches of Buena Vista Creek.

3.0 Cross the East Fork of Redwood Creek.

3.5 Cross a creek below a small waterfall.

4.7 Admire the Fallen Goliath.

5.2 Cross Redwood Creek and make a right.

5.3 Pass the Sugarbowl Trail and continue straight.

6.9 Meet the Hart Tree Trail junction and turn left.

7.2 Arrive back at the trailhead.

12 Big Baldy Ridge

This trip takes you to a striking 360–degree view of Kings Canyon and Sequoia National Parks from the summit of Big Baldy. It continues on to a less–visited view of the west face of Chimney Rock.

Distance: 5.6 miles out and back
Approximate hiking time: 4 hours
Difficulty: More challenging, due to elevation gain
Trail surface: Dirt
Canine compatibility: Dogs not permitted
Fees and permits: Park entrance fee; no permit required
Best season: June through Oct
Maps: USGS General Grant Grove
Trail contacts: Sequoia and Kings Canyon National Parks, 47050 Generals Hwy., Three Rivers, CA 93271-9700; (559) 565-3341; www.nps.gov/seki; Grant Grove Visitor Center, 3 miles east of the Big Stump entrance station
Special considerations: There are no restrooms or water at this trailhead. If you see dark clouds nearby, hear thunder, or observe hail, rain, or static electricity in the air, descend immediately. There are steep drop-offs around the summit; exercise caution.

Finding the trailhead: From the Big Stump entrance station, drive east on CA 180 to the junction with the Generals Highway at 1.2 miles and make a right. Drive south for 5.6 miles to the signed parking turnout on the southwest side of a large, blind curve just west of Big Meadows Road. If the parking area is full, another large turnout is available on the south side of the road, a little farther to the east. The trailhead is located on the southwest side of the parking area. GPS: N36 41.51 / W118 52.43

The Hike

The trail enters the forest and meets a trail from the Montecito Sequoia Lodge. The Montecito Trail is on private property; unless you are a guest at the lodge, do not enter the area. The Big Baldy Ridge Trail winds between large boulders, chinquapin, and snowbrush beneath tall firs and pines. Ascend through an open, rocky area edged with manzanita, then go back into the woods. The route dips slightly and climbs again, passing many colorful wildflowers, notably skyrockets and penstemons in summer.

Entering another granitic area, you round a small dome and proceed up the ridge. As the trail levels a bit, a view of the summit opens up to the south. Reenter the trees and rise again, soon reaching a penstemon-lined switchback. The trail contours around the east side of the high point, just below the ridge crest. As the trail swings up toward the summit, you pass a notch in the ridge that gives you a glimpse of the extreme drop-off.

At 2.1 miles you reach the summit of Big Baldy (8,209 feet). The views are spectacular. To the north are Nelson Mountain and Eagle Peak near Courtright Reservoir, Spanish Mountain, Obelisk, Castle Peak, Mount Goddard, and jagged peaks in northern Kings Canyon National Park. Nearest to you, in the north, is Buena Vista Peak. To the east the Great Western Divide and the Kaweah Peaks serve as a backdrop for Mount Silliman and Alta Peak. To the southeast are the peaks surrounding Mineral King, including Sawtooth Peak. To the west, Redwood Canyon, Redwood Mountain, and the smog-shrouded San Joaquin Valley are visible.

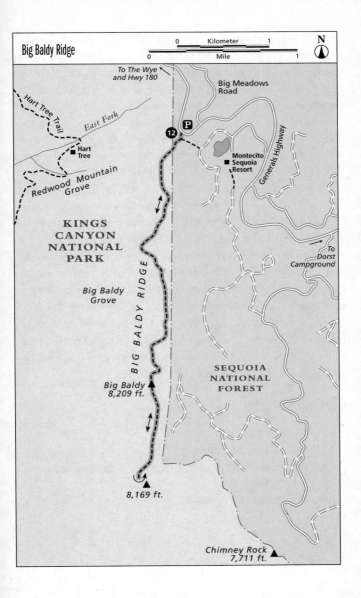

Leaving the summit, the trail continues south, along the west side of the short, stout summit pinnacles. It leads down, around the east side of the next dome, through rocky terrain. You descend to a saddle with a view of a pond and a meadow in the Pierce Valley to the west, and of the Sunrise Bowl just below you to the east. A metal-roofed structure and radio tower are located here. The path rounds another dome and travels through open forest to reach a portion of trail completely covered by crushed rock.

Your path then enters a forested area with many birds, including nuthatches, western bluebirds, and western tanagers. As you climb out of the forest, watch for a nice view of Chimney Rock and Little Baldy through the trees. The trail ascends, winding through talus blocks on the west side of a lower outcrop of Big Baldy Ridge at 2.8 miles. At an elevation of 8,169 feet, the views to the east of Chimney Rock and Little Baldy are exceptional; the Great Western Divide looms in the background. To the west are lower Redwood Canyon, Eshom Valley, and the San Joaquin Valley. Enjoy the views before backtracking to the parking area at 5.6 miles.

Miles and Directions

0.0 Start at the trailhead.

2.1 Attain the Big Baldy summit.

2.8 Reach a second high point, with a view of Chimney Rock. Retrace your steps.

5.6 Arrive back at the trailhead.

Hikes in the Cedar Grove Area

13 **Roaring River Falls to Zumwalt Meadow**

From billowing Roaring River Falls to peaceful Zumwalt Meadow, this hike is ideal for a picnic lunch or just relaxing.

Distance: 3.9-mile lollipop
Approximate hiking time: 2 hours
Difficulty: Easy
Trail surface: Some paved; dirt
Canine compatibility: Dogs not permitted
Fees and permits: Park entrance fee; no permit required
Best season: Late May through Oct
Maps: USGS The Sphinx; Kings Canyon National Park Cedar Grove (available at park visitor centers)

Trail contacts: Sequoia and Kings Canyon National Parks, 47050 Generals Hwy., Three Rivers, CA 93271-9700; (559) 565-3341; www.nps.gov/seki; Cedar Grove Visitor Center, 29 miles from Grant Grove on CA 180.

Special considerations: There are no restrooms or water available at this trailhead. An interpretive pamphlet for the Zumwalt Meadow Trail can be purchased at its parking area and at park visitor centers. The trail begins on the south side of the parking area, east of the bridge.

Finding the trailhead: On CA 180, drive approximately 32 miles north, then east, of Grant Grove. Continue past Cedar Grove to the Roaring River Falls parking area on the right (south). Parking is available on the south side of the highway on either side of the bridge spanning the Roaring River. GPS: N36 47.1 / W118 37.20

The Hike

The paved trail begins by following the Roaring River. In a few hundred feet you reach the River Trail, your route to Zumwalt Meadow. For now, continue straight ahead (south) to the falls at 0.1 mile.

As you approach the overlook, you will hear the roar of rushing water plunging into the blue-green pool that fills this granite bowl. Shrubs and small trees cling to the cliffs, which seem to reach straight up to the sky. When the falls are at their peak, mist douses those standing at the overlook. Only the lower portion of Roaring River Falls is visible; the upper cascades are inaccessible. (Do not venture up the canyon on side trails. Others have been injured or killed trying to do so.)

After enjoying the falls safely, backtrack to the River Trail junction at 0.2 mile and make a right (east) turn. The rocky, open trail travels close to the road at first but soon enters a shady forest along the South Fork of the Kings River. Continue on through the forest and clearings laced with the scent of incense cedar. After climbing a couple of rocky knolls, you come to the suspension bridge that leads to the Zumwalt Meadow Trail parking area, where an interpretive pamphlet can be purchased, at 1.6 miles.

Continue straight (east), and cross the usually dry Sentinel Creek—be prepared to rock-hop if the creek is flowing. Meet the Zumwalt Meadow Trail junction at 1.7 miles. Turn left (northeast) and cross a seasonal creek on a small footbridge. North Dome and Lion Head rise above the trees to the north, while the Grand Sentinel towers above the meadow to the south.

Roaring River Falls to Zumwalt Meadow

The trail travels along a boardwalk through the fragile meadow, then enters a shady forest while following the Kings River. Pause to enjoy the many tree-framed views of the meadow, accompanied by the peaceful splashing and rippling of the river. You may see a hummingbird, a dipper, or even a deer if the trail is not crowded.

Two spur trails on your left (east) connect with the River Trail as the path begins to leave the forest. After passing between two large boulders, the route reaches the main junction with the River Trail at 2.3 miles. Turn right (west) and begin a short climb. With Zumwalt Meadow visible below, the trail winds through a moonscape of talus blocks at the base of the Grand Sentinel. The trail dips, rises again, and recrosses the seasonal creek.

At 2.5 miles you reach the Zumwalt Meadow Trail junction and complete the loop portion of the trip. Retrace your steps on the remainder of your journey, returning to Roaring River parking area at 3.9 miles.

Miles and Directions

0.0 Start at the trailhead.

0.1 Check out Roaring River Falls.

0.2 Return to the River Trail junction and make a right.

1.6 Pass the suspension bridge and continue straight.

1.7 Meet the Zumwalt Meadow Trail and turn left.

2.3 Arrive at the River Trail junction and make a right.

2.5 Pass the Zumwalt Meadow Trail junction and continue straight ahead.

3.8 Return to the Roaring River Falls Trail junction and turn right.

3.9 Arrive back at the trailhead.

14 Mist Falls

This outing takes you to delightful Mist Falls, a wonderful place for a picnic lunch in the shade.

Distance: 8.2 miles out and back

Approximate hiking time: 5 hours

Difficulty: Moderate, due to length

Trail surface: Dirt

Best season: Mid-June through Oct

Other trail users: Equestrians

Canine compatibility: Dogs not permitted

Fees and permits: Park entrance fee; no permit required

Maps: USGS The Sphinx; Kings Canyon National Park Cedar Grove (available at park visitor centers)

Trail contacts: Sequoia and Kings Canyon National Parks, 47050 Generals Hwy., Three Rivers, CA 93271-9700; (559) 565-3341; www.nps.gov/seki; Cedar Grove Visitor Center, 29 miles from Grant Grove on CA 180.

Special considerations: Restrooms, a water spigot, and an information center are located at the east end of the day-use parking area. This trail can be very hot; be sure to get an early start. Mountain lions frequent this area. You are advised not to hike solo.

Finding the trailhead: Follow CA 180 north, then east, for approximately 29 miles from Grant Grove to Cedar Grove. The trailhead is approximately 6.6 miles past Cedar Grove Village at the Road's End parking area. The trail begins at the information center. GPS: N36 47.42 / W118 34.59

The Hike

The Paradise Valley Trail starts at the information center and travels through sunny woods. Cross the Copper Creek Bridge; the bridge is north of the Kanawyer's Store site, which served cattlemen and sheepherders heading into the backcountry in the early days. John Muir had even visited the old supply point, but it was torn down in the late 1920s. The Cedar Grove Ranger Station displays a picture of the store during its heyday.

Several side trails lead down to the river on the right (south), while the Grand Sentinel towers above on the south side of the canyon. Large gray squirrels scamper about, especially in the fall, when they are gathering acorns and pinecones for the winter. The path advances through manzanita clearings in the pockets of forest, then crosses a rocky knoll. Enter a shady area thick with green horsetails and reach a trail junction at 2.1 miles. To the right (south), the Bubbs Creek Trail leads across a Bailey bridge. Continue straight ahead (northeast) and uphill.

Soon you gain a view of the confluence of Bubbs Creek. The path dips and rises through the shade of cedars, oaks, and firs, with an understory of ferns and horsetails as it passes below Buck Peak. When you have climbed and switchbacked through mixed forest, a view of The Sphinx opens up down the canyon behind you. The path ascends a bit more, with views of lacy cascades on the river below, before reaching the deluge of Mist Falls at 4.1 miles. In early season a cool mist wafts through the air, making this a wonderfully refreshing rest stop.

Watch your step in this area—the rocks near the falls are slippery and dangerous. After you have enjoyed your destination, retrace your steps to the parking area at 8.2 miles.

Miles and Directions

- **0.0** Start at the trailhead.
- **2.1** The trail forks; continue straight ahead.
- **4.1** Arrive at Mist Falls. When ready, return the way you came.
- **8.2** Arrive back at the trailhead.

Hikes in the Mineral King and South Fork Areas

15 Cold Springs Nature Trail

This easy ramble takes you through meadows and aspen groves along the East Fork of the Kaweah River, giving you nice views of the surrounding peaks. It also leads to the former site of the mining settlement of Beulah.

Distance: 2.0 miles out and back

Approximate hiking time: 1 hour

Difficulty: Easy

Trail surface: Dirt

Best season: June through Oct

Canine compatibility: Dogs not permitted

Fees and permits: Park entrance fee; no permit required

Maps: Sequoia National Park Mineral King (the trail is not shown on other maps), available at park visitor centers

Trail contacts: Sequoia and Kings Canyon National Parks, 47050 Generals Hwy., Three Rivers, CA 93271-9700; (559) 565-3341; www.nps.gov/seki; Mineral King Ranger Station, 24 miles from CA 198, on Mineral King Road

Special considerations: Restrooms are located at the picnic area; water is available in the Cold Springs Campground.

Finding the trailhead: From central Three Rivers, drive north on CA 198 for approximately 3.9 miles to Mineral King Road. Turn right (east) and follow the road for 10.1 miles to the Lookout Point entrance station. Continue east, passing Atwell Mill Campground, then Cabin Cove and the Silver City Store and Resort at 20.5 miles. Reach the Mineral King Ranger Station at 24 miles. Park at the picnic area on the south side of the road, across from the ranger station, or at the small turnout across from the Cold Springs Campground entrance. From the picnic area, follow the road west to the Cold Springs Campground entrance and a small parking turnout. Turn left (south). Cross the bridge and turn left again, now heading east.

The signed nature trail begins next to Campsite 6. GPS: N36 27.5 / W118 36.41

The Hike

The trail begins by passing through an open, grassy area filled with meadow goldenrod, Bigelow's sneezeweed, and many other wildflowers in summer. You come to the first interpretive sign as you enter cottonwoods and aspens. The interpretive signs identify the native plants and trees growing in the Mineral King Valley. When the trail forks, take the path to the left (east); the other path is part of your return trip. Pass the junction with the other portion of the interpretive trail and continue straight ahead, passing a couple of nice places to rest or eat lunch along the river.

The trail climbs briefly over a small rise, then dips to cross two small brooks on plank bridges in a hillside meadow. Enjoy the nice view down to the sparkling East Fork of the Kaweah River below as the path climbs a couple of switchbacks and enters a grove of firs. The trail then dips to cross a boggy hillside meadow watered by Iron Spring. Sierra gentians bloom profusely here in late summer. Ahead of you and across the valley is Black Wolf Falls, with Empire Mountain and Sawtooth Peak towering above.

The flat area of sagebrush that follows has views of Florence and Tulare Peaks to the south. At 0.8 mile you will reach the site of the New England smelter, just before a grove of aspen. Some foundation supports are all that is left of the smelter, which was used in the late 1800s.

Mineral Peak becomes visible to the right (south) of Sawtooth Peak prior to entering the aspen grove. The route winds through sagebrush mixed with flowers, and Rainbow Mountain joins Florence and Tulare Peaks and Farewell

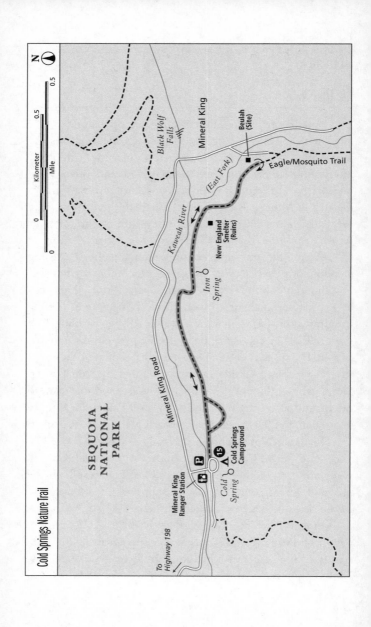

Cold Springs Nature Trail

SEQUOIA NATIONAL PARK

To Highway 198

Mineral King Road

Mineral King Ranger Station

Cold Spring

Cold Springs Campground

Iron Spring

New England Smelter (Ruins)

Kaweah River

(East Fork)

Black Wolf Falls

Mineral King

Beulah (Site)

Eagle/Mosquito Trail

N

Kilometer   0.5

Mile   0.5

Gap in your view to the south. Proceed through a private residential area near tall fir trees. At 1.0 mile, arrive at the small sign marking the site of Beulah, a community that thrived during Mineral King's mining days. An avalanche set off by the San Francisco earthquake of 1906 leveled most of Beulah. Now private cabins occupy the town site.

The road ahead leads down to the Eagle-Mosquito parking area, passing through private cabins, each signed with family names and the year it was built. If you venture down to the parking area, stay on the road and respect the private property.

When you are ready to return, retrace your steps to the trail fork at 1.8 miles and turn left (south) to travel the other portion of the interpretive trail. You will arrive at the trailhead at 2.0 miles.

Miles and Directions

0.0 Start at the trailhead, next to Campsite 6.

0.2 Meet the nature loop and take the fork to the left.

0.8 Reach the smelter ruins.

1.0 Reach the site of Beulah; retrace your steps to the trail junction of the nature loop.

1.8 Meet the nature loop and take the fork to the left.

2.0 Arrive back at the trailhead.

16 White Chief Canyon

This trek to a magnificent alpine bowl passes two waterfalls, the ruins of a cabin, an expansive meadow, mine shafts, and marble caverns along the way.

Distance: 8.2 miles out and back
Approximate hiking time: 5.5 hours
Difficulty: More challenging, due to length and elevation gain
Trail surface: Dirt
Best season: July through Sept
Other trail users: Equestrians
Canine compatibility: Dogs not permitted
Fees and permits: Park entrance fee; no permit required
Maps: USGS Mineral King; Sequoia National Park Mineral King (available at park visitor centers)

Trail contacts: Sequoia and Kings Canyon National Parks, 47050 Generals Hwy., Three Rivers, CA 93271-9700; (559) 565-3341; www.nps.gov/seki; Mineral King Ranger Station, 24 miles from CA 198, on Mineral King Road
Special considerations: The trailhead has a "Charge a Call" phone but no restrooms or water. The nearest restrooms are located at the Sawtooth Pass parking area or across the road from the Mineral King Ranger Station.

Finding the trailhead: From central Three Rivers, drive north on CA 198 for approximately 3.9 miles to Mineral King Road. Turn right (east) and follow the road for 10.1 miles to the Lookout Point entrance station. Continue east, passing Atwell Mill Campground, then Cabin Cove and the Silver City Store and Resort at 20.5 miles. Reach the Mineral King Ranger Station at 24 miles. The parking area is 1.3 miles farther down the road, to the right and across a wooden bridge. Pass the Sawtooth Pass parking area and a junction with a dirt road leading to the pack station on the way. The trail begins at the south end of the parking area. GPS: N36 26.59 / W118 35.43

The Hike

The trail begins with a slight ascent, passing the restored Honeymoon Cabin. At 0.3 mile you cross Spring Creek on a wooden footbridge below Tufa Falls, which comes from a spring high above you on the canyon wall. The Farewell Gap Trail is visible across the canyon, along the east bank of the East Fork of the Kaweah River.

After the creek crossing, a horse trail from the pack station across the river joins your route. Look east for a view up the cascades of Crystal Creek, tumbling down to the right (south) of Mineral Peak. Tulare Peak is to the southeast; the silver ribbon to its left (north) is Franklin Creek. Look to the north to see Timber Gap and Empire Mountain high above the valley floor.

After stepping through the shallow waters of Eagle Creek at 0.9 mile, the climb steepens. At 1.0 mile you reach the Eagle-Mosquito Trail junction; continue straight (south) up the steep path. The route nears White Chief Creek, which is lined with blocks of metamorphic stone. Travel through jagged rock, and reach the usually dry crossing of the creek at 2.0 miles. Due to the porous nature of the marble in this area, White Chief Creek flows underground in some places. The meager ruins of Crabtree Cabin are to the right (west), just before the creek crossing.

The path follows the edge of White Chief Meadow, which is closed in by towering granite walls. It then climbs through forest, passing a primitive camping area on the right (west). When the trail leaves the trees, a pretty waterfall comes into view at the lower portion of the canyon. As you near the waterfall, look west across the canyon to the right of White Chief Peak; you can spot the creek trickling down

White Chief Canyon

Kilometer

Mile

N

To Ranger
Station

Mineral King
Road

Honeymoon
Cabin

Cold Springs
Campground

Pack Station,
Corral

Spring
Creek

Tufa
Falls

Miners
Nose

SEQUOIA
NATIONAL
PARK

Kaweah River (East Fork)

Crystal Creek

Mosquito Lakes Trail

Eagle
Sinkholes

Aspen
Flat

Soda
Spring

First
Mosquito
Lake

Miner's Ridge

Eagle Creek

White Chief Creek

Franklin Creek

Mosquito
Lakes

Crabtree Cabin
(Ruins)

Concrete
Dam

White Chief Canyon

Eagle
Lake

White Chief
Lake

White Chief Mine

White Chief
Peak

White Chief
Bowl

from White Chief Lake. A footpath continues to the base of the falls. Your route is the dim track that splits off to the right (west), leading down to a rock-hop of White Chief Creek and the continuation of the trail.

At 2.9 miles the route passes several shafts of the White Chief Mine (which is private property) as it switchbacks through marble and other metamorphic rock. At the upper bench of the canyon, you pass sinkholes and marble caverns before another usually dry crossing of the creek. Do not attempt to enter any of the mine shafts or caverns; such exploring is very dangerous!

At the next junction, the right (west) fork leads to the ruins of a cavern-turned-homestead and to a large sinkhole. Take the left (south) fork to White Chief Bowl. After passing through overgrown willows, you arrive at the canyon's end. Steep rock walls, verdant meadows, and a small tarn await you at 4.1 miles. Hummingbirds flit overhead, while Vandever Mountain towers above to the left (southeast) in dark and brooding colors. When you have enjoyed the alpine scene, return the way you came (8.2 miles).

Miles and Directions

0.0   Start at the trailhead.

0.3   Cross Spring Creek below Tufa Falls.

0.9   Ford the shallow waters of Eagle Creek.

1.0   Reach a trail junction with the Eagle-Mosquito Trail and continue straight ahead.

2.0   Cross White Chief Creek at the Crabtree Cabin ruins.

2.9   Recross White Chief Creek below the White Chief Mine.

4.1   Reach White Chief Bowl. When ready, retrace your steps.

8.2   Arrive back at the trailhead.

17 First Mosquito Lake

This hike makes a nice trip to a pretty lake, perfect for a picnic lunch with time to relax on the shore.

Distance: 7.2 miles out and back

Approximate hiking time: 4.5 hours

Difficulty: More challenging, due to elevation gain

Trail surface: Dirt

Best season: July through Sept

Other trail users: Equestrians

Canine compatibility: Dogs not permitted

Fees and permits: Park entrance fee; no permit required

Maps: USGS Mineral King; Sequoia National Park Mineral King (available at park visitor centers)

Trail contacts: Sequoia and Kings Canyon National Parks, 47050 Generals Hwy., Three Rivers, CA 93271-9700; (559) 565-3341; www.nps.gov/seki; Mineral King Ranger Station, 24 miles from CA 198, on Mineral King Road.

Special considerations: The trailhead has a "Charge a Call" phone but no restrooms or water. The nearest restrooms are located at the Sawtooth Pass parking area or across the road from the Mineral King Ranger Station.

Finding the trailhead: From central Three Rivers, drive north on CA 198 for approximately 3.9 miles to Mineral King Road. Turn right (east) and follow the road for 10.1 miles to the Lookout Point entrance station. Continue east, passing Atwell Mill Campground, then Cabin Cove and the Silver City Store and Resort at 20.5 miles. Reach the Mineral King Ranger Station at 24 miles. The parking area is 1.3 miles farther down the road, to the right and across a wooden bridge. Pass the Sawtooth Pass parking area and a junction with a dirt road leading to the pack station on the way. The trail begins at the south end of the parking area. GPS: N36 26.59 / W118 35.43

The Hike

Begin by following the trail to White Chief Canyon. The trail begins with a slight ascent, passing the restored Honeymoon Cabin. You cross Spring Creek on a wooden bridge at 0.3 mile and reach the Eagle-Mosquito Trail junction at 1.0 mile. Turn right (west). As you ascend steep switchbacks, the pack station appears diminutive far below. The route continues to climb, bringing you through a thick patch of woods to a steeply sloped meadow and more switchbacks.

Leveling off, the trail follows the dry canyon of Eagle Creek before arriving at the Eagle Sinkholes. Here Eagle Creek disappears into a large, deep crater and flows underground, leaving its former streambed dry. Another sinkhole can be found farther down the one-time watercourse. It is possible that Spring Creek, which you crossed earlier, receives its water from a subterranean stream originating in this area.

A few more switchbacks and you reach the Mosquito Lakes Trail junction at 2.0 miles. Turn right (northwest). The trail passes through a grassy meadow before winding up the slope. As you pass by the talus, watch for pikas, a tiny animal related to the rabbit. The views across Mineral King Valley to Sawtooth and Mineral Peaks in the east are breathtaking. Behind you and to the south is dark and craggy Vandever Mountain.

The path steadily ascends Miner's Ridge through a shady fir forest. Switchbacks up give way to short switchbacks down, and you descend through purple lupine to reach the first Mosquito Lake at 3.6 miles. Camping is not allowed at this lake, but it makes a good place to take a lunch break.

First Mosquito Lake

To Hwy 198

Mineral King Ranger Station

Mineral King Road

Mineral King

New England Smelter (Ruins)

Cold Springs Campground

Cold Spring

Beulah (Site)

17

Honeymoon Cabin

Pack Station, Corral

SEQUOIA NATIONAL PARK

Miners Nose

Spring Creek

Tufa Falls

Mosquito Creek

Mosquito Lakes Trail

Kaweah River (East Fork)

First Mosquito Lake

Miner's Ridge

Eagle Sinkholes

Eagle Creek

Mosquito Lakes

Crabtree Cabin (Ruins)

Concrete Dam

Eagle Lake

Kilometer 0.5

Mile 0.5

N

When you have finished exploring the lake, retrace your steps over Miner's Ridge and return to the parking area at 7.2 miles.

Option

An unmaintained trail crosses the lake's outlet, passing a much steeper unmaintained route that leads down Mosquito Creek to Cold Springs Campground. You can easily take the unmaintained trail from the outlet to the south side of the lake. Beyond, the path becomes more rugged and harder to follow as it leads to the other Mosquito lakes.

Miles and Directions

0.0 Start at the trailhead.
0.3 Cross Spring Creek below Tufa Falls.
1.0 Reach the Eagle-Mosquito Trail junction and make a right.
2.0 Reach the Mosquito Lakes Trail junction and make another right.
3.6 Arrive at the first Mosquito Lake. Retrace your steps.
7.2 Arrive back at the trailhead.

18 Ladybug Camp

This trip follows the first portion of the historic Hockett Trail, a trans–Sierra route built in the 1860s. The destination is a flat where ladybugs winter along the South Fork of the Kaweah River.

Distance: 3.8 miles out and back

Approximate hiking time: 4.5 hours

Difficulty: Moderate

Trail surface: Dirt

Best season: Mid-March through May; Oct through mid-Nov

Canine compatibility: Dogs not permitted

Fees and permits: No entrance fee; no permit required

Maps: USGS Dennison Peak and Moses Mountain

Trail contacts: Sequoia and Kings Canyon National Parks, 47050 Generals Hwy., Three Rivers, CA 93271-9700; (559) 565-3341; www.nps.gov/seki

Special considerations: Restrooms are located in the South Fork Campground. Mountain lions frequent this area. You are advised not to hike solo.

Finding the trailhead: From central Three Rivers, follow South Fork Drive southeast, then east, to the Sequoia National Park boundary, where you lose the pavement. Continue on the dirt road to South Fork Campground, approximately 13 miles total. Day-use parking is west of the campground. Overnight parking is located farther down the road, east of the campground, at the trailhead. The trail begins at the east end of the overnight parking area. GPS: N36 20.59 / W118 45.47

The Hike

The trail sets off along the south bluff of the South Fork of the Kaweah River and then crosses the river on a long wooden footbridge. On the other side, the trail climbs briefly. At 0.3 mile a dim side trail to the left (north) leads to Clough Cave, home to a colony of endangered bats. The side trail rises uphill, becoming narrow and washed out just before the cave. Bars have been installed at the entrance due to the vandalism this cave has suffered.

The main route leads east along a rocky trail, through the shade of oaks and cedars. Watch out for the abundant poison oak. Side trails branch off toward the river, and a long-abandoned trail climbs to Salt Creek Ridge just before you reach the rarely flowing Pigeon Creek at 0.5 mile.

Continue east, traversing high above the river on rocky shelves. Look south across the canyon for a view of a waterfall on Putnam Creek. The trail curves into the canyon of Squaw Creek and crosses the watercourse on a small log at 1.0 mile. The path then swings back to the southeast, with views across the South Fork to Dennison Ridge. Flat areas appear along the river below, and you reach a signed junction above Ladybug Camp at 1.9 miles.

Follow a footpath down to Ladybug Camp, where you can find wintering ladybugs on the underside of fallen leaves during the cooler months of the hiking season. Be careful not to harm them as you explore. When you have returned to the junction, follow the east-trending path to its demise at the river. The metal stakes that stick up through the granite mark the site of an old bridge, which collapsed in 1969 due to an exceptionally heavy snowpack.

On the other side of the river is the continuation of the historic Hockett Trail, which was constructed to transport supplies to the silver mines on the east side of the Sierra Nevada. It is now quite overgrown up to the point where it joins the Garfield-Hockett Trail, which also leads into the

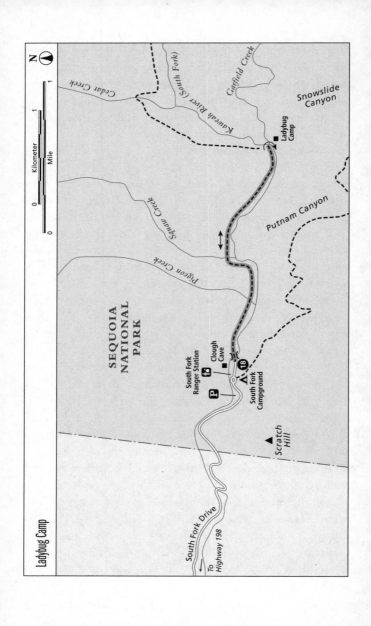

Ladybug Camp

backcountry. Across the river, near the confluence of Garfield Creek, stands a solitary sequoia growing at one of the lowest elevations at which a sequoia is known to grow. It is thought that, as a seedling, this tree was washed down the slope from the Garfield Grove in an 1876 landslide.

After enjoying the area, return the way you came and reach the trailhead at 3.8 miles.

Miles and Directions

0.0 Start at the trailhead.

0.3 A side trail leads to Clough Cave; make a right.

0.5 Cross Pigeon Creek.

1.0 Cross the log over Squaw Creek.

1.9 Reach Ladybug Camp and explore. When ready, head back the way you came.

3.8 Arrive back at the trailhead.

Hikes in the Jennie Lakes Wilderness

19 Mitchell Peak

This trip takes you to a spectacular 360–degree vista on top of a windswept 10,365–foot peak, the site of a former fire lookout tower.

Distance: 6.4 miles out and back

Approximate hiking time: 5 hours

Difficulty: More challenging, due to elevation gain

Trail surface: Dirt

Best season: Mid-June through Oct

Other trail users: Equestrians, cattle

Canine compatibility: Leashed dogs permitted

Fees and permits: Park entrance fee; no permit required

Maps: USGS Muir Grove; USFS Monarch and Jennie Lakes Wilderness (available at Sequoia National Forest visitor centers, the national forest Web site, and sporting goods stores)

Trail contacts: Sequoia National Forest, Hume Lake RD, 35860 East Kings Canyon Rd., Dunlap, CA 93621; (559) 338-2251; www.fs.fed.us/r5/sequoia; ranger station open Mon through Fri

Special considerations: There are no restrooms or water at this trailhead. The nearest restrooms are at the Big Meadows trailhead, 7.8 miles back down FR 14S11. During storms, there is a risk of being struck by lightning on the summit of Mitchell Peak. If you see dark clouds nearby, hear thunder, or observe hail, rain, or static electricity in the air, descend immediately.

Finding the trailhead: From the Big Stump entrance station, drive east on CA 180 to the junction with the Generals Highway at 1.2 miles and make a right. Drive south for 5.8 miles to FR 14S11 to Big Meadows, which is just beyond the Big Baldy trailhead. Turn left (northeast) and follow the road past the historic ranger cabin (which is now a rental), Big Meadows trailhead, and the campgrounds. The road narrows, crosses Big Meadows Creek, and passes a few spur roads before entering a deep canyon and crossing Boulder Creek at a large curve. Pass the road signed for the Horse Corral pack station, Sunset Meadow, and Rowell Meadow trailhead, and cross Horse Corral Creek. At 18.3 miles you will reach the second dirt road on the right, FR 13S12, signed for Marvin Pass trailhead. Turn right (south) and follow the rough dirt road, passing several spur roads. It is easy to distinguish the main road until you reach the last unsigned spur road. It continues straight ahead (east, leading to private property), while you turn right (south) on FR 13S12, following the well-used road to its end at the trailhead parking area at 20.6 miles. The trail begins at the south end of the parking area. GPS: N36 44.27 / W118 44.17

The Hike

The Forest Service trail, FS 30E43, follows an abandoned logging road for just a few feet before abruptly turning south at a wooden trail sign. The dusty path climbs to cross a ridge, turns east, and passes through a level logged area where currants, manzanita, and snowbrush grow. Marvin Pass is the low wooded gap to the right (south). A trail that leads to private property joins your route at 0.2 mile.

Turning south again, you rock-hop a small brook and skirt a meadow clipped short by grazing cattle. The trail ascends several switchbacks. You may notice a horse trail to your right, which comes up from one of the spur roads you passed on your drive to the trailhead. The trail crests timbered Marvin Pass at 1.0 mile and reaches a trail junction while entering the Jennie Lakes Wilderness. This is a good place to rest and refuel.

The Marvin Pass Trail continues straight (south), downhill and on to Rowell Meadow. Take the trail to the left (east) and follow FS 30E07 between two large boulders toward Mitchell Peak. The route rises and dips, passing through shady forest and dry, sunny slopes dotted with lupine and red skyrockets. Meadows are visible here and there, below you on the right.

At 1.7 miles you reach the Mitchell Peak Trail, FS 30E07A, and turn left (northeast). The route climbs gradually at first. When it comes to a clearing you can see your destination—the rocky mountaintop on your right (east).

The path ascends more steeply and crosses the western ridge emanating from the peak. When the grade lessens, Horse Corral Meadow, where the last grizzly bear in California was shot in 1922, is visible through the trees, downhill to the left (northwest). As the slope becomes steep again, the trail turns to the south and winds up through a thinning forest of foxtail pines and an understory of lupines and phlox. When you reach the granite blocks, follow ducks (rock cairns) up through the talus that caps the peak. Some maneuvering through the blocks is necessary to attain the summit; go slowly and carefully.

Upon reaching a mostly level area, you will see a pinnacle a few feet ahead of you at 3.2 miles. This is the high point of Mitchell Peak. If you do not wish to climb up to this roost, you can still see the entire view by making your way to the west and east sides of the mountaintop. A concrete slab on the west side of the summit is all that is left of the Mitchell Peak Lookout, but it still provides a good spot to take in the views in all directions. A granite balcony on the east side of the pinnacle makes a great place to take in the views to the east and southeast.

To the northwest, the canyon of the Kings River, Spanish Mountain, and Obelisk are set against the backdrop of

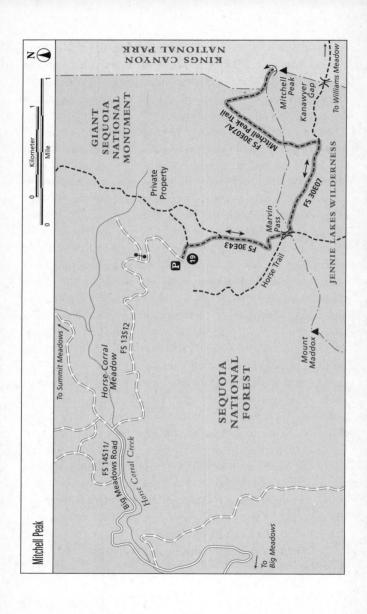

the John Muir Wilderness. On a clear day, you can see Dogtooth Peak in the Dinkey Lakes Wilderness. To the north are the Monarch Divide, Mount Goddard, and northern Kings Canyon National Park, and to the northeast is the headwaters country of the Kings River and Middle Palisade on the Sierra Crest. East of you is the Great Western Divide, with Sugarloaf and Sugarloaf Valley down below. The Kaweahs tower above all else to the southeast, and the Tablelands, Mount Silliman, Twin Peaks, and Kettle Peak fill the view to the south. Looking from the southwest to the west, you can see Poop Out Pass, Shell Mountain, Rowell Meadow, Mount Maddox, and even Buck Rock Lookout.

After you have delighted in this spectacular vista, return to the trailhead at 6.4 miles.

Miles and Directions

0.0 Start at the trailhead.

0.2 Pass a trail to private property; turn right.

1.0 Crest Marvin Pass; take the trail to the left.

1.7 Meet the Mitchell Peak Trail and turn left.

3.2 Reach the top of Mitchell Peak and take in the views. Retrace your steps.

6.4 Arrive back at the trailhead.

20 Weaver Lake

This enjoyable hike takes you to a striking lake, warm enough for swimming, at the base of Shell Mountain. The views along the way are superior.

Distance: 6.4 miles out and back

Approximate hiking time: 4 hours

Difficulty: Moderate, due to elevation gain

Trail surface: Dirt

Best season: June through Oct

Other trail users: Equestrians, cattle, mountain bikers to wilderness boundary

Canine compatibility: Leashed dogs permitted

Maps: USGS Muir Grove; USFS Monarch and Jennie Lakes

Wilderness (available at Sequoia National Forest visitor centers, the national forest Web site, and sporting goods stores)

Trail contacts: Sequoia National Forest, Hume Lake RD, 35860 East Kings Canyon Rd., Dunlap, CA 93621; (559) 338-2251; www.fs.fed.us/r5/sequoia; ranger station open Mon through Fri

Special considerations: A restroom is located at this trailhead, but there is no water.

Finding the trailhead: From the Big Stump entrance station, drive east on CA 180 to the junction with the Generals Highway at 1.2 miles and make a right. Drive south for 5.8 miles to FR 14S11 to Big Meadows, which is just beyond the Big Baldy trailhead. Turn left (northeast) and follow the road past the ranger station. The Big Meadows trailhead parking area is on the right (south) before the campground at 12.9 miles. GPS: N36 43.3 / W118 50.1

The Hike

The trail, FS 29E05, leads downhill, skirting the camp-ground to cross Big Meadows Creek on a collapsed wooden footbridge and reach a four-way junction. A fisherman's trail heads south along the creek, and a footpath/cow trail leads uphill straight ahead, then over to Big Meadows. Your route is the well-worn path to the left (east), which soon comes to a trail register.

The trail travels uphill, around a granitic ridge, and follows an unnamed creek before crossing it at 0.6 mile. Climb to an open, sunny area where a side trail branches off to the left (northeast); it heads toward a barren ridgetop before rejoining the rocky main route. Your path reenters the forest and rises to cross a ridge. You soon have a view to the north of Spanish Mountain, the Obelisk, and the Monarch Divide.

Another side trail, this time branching to the right (south), leads uphill and back to rejoin the main route. The trail descends to meet an unmapped pathway, leading up from FR 14S16, at beautiful Fox Meadow at 1.4 miles.

Wind around this patch of green surrounded by dense woodland and then ascend through the thinning trees. At 1.8 miles you reach the junction with the trail to Jennie Lake. Go left (northeast) onto FS 30E06 and immediately step across a creek tumbling down from a small, unnamed lake near the base of Shell Mountain.

Enter the Jennie Lakes Wilderness; the climb lessens a bit as the trail becomes rockier. You may see the top of Shell Mountain peeking over the trees. The route spans a seasonal creek as well as the sometimes dry Weaver Creek,

Weaver Lake

then arrives at trail signs and the short path to Weaver Lake on your right (southeast) at 3.0 miles.

A brief clamber through a rocky obstacle course deposits you on the shores of Weaver Lake at 3.2 miles, below the rugged face of Shell Mountain. There are campsites along the grassy shores and a large one just north of the lake, which is visible from the trail. Wild blueberries grow in the forest surrounding the lake. After relishing the scenery, or perhaps going for a swim, retrace your steps to the trailhead at 6.4 miles.

Miles and Directions

0.0 Start at the trailhead.

0.6 Cross an unnamed creek.

1.4 Pass an unmapped trail and continue straight.

1.8 Reach the Jennie Lake Trail junction; turn left.

3.0 Arrive at the Weaver Lake Trail fork; make a right.

3.2 Reach the shores of Weaver Lake. Retrace your steps.

6.4 Arrive back at the trailhead.

Clubs and Trail Groups

Sierra Club
Tehipite Chapter
P.O. Box 5396
Fresno, CA 93755-5396
(559) 229-4031 (message only)
http://tehipite.sierraclub.org
The Sierra Club works to promote conservation and protect our natural areas. Members can attend guided hiking trips, some in Sequoia and Kings Canyon National Parks.

Fresno Audubon Society
P.O. Box 9324
Fresno, CA 93791-9324
(559) 222-2473
www.fresnoaudubon.org
The Audubon Society promotes the preservation of birds and wildlife, as well as their habitats. Members can attend hiking trips for bird watching, some in Sequoia and Kings Canyon National Parks.

About the Author

Laurel Scheidt, born and raised in the central San Joaquin Valley, considers the Sierra Nevada her home away from home. She has traveled many of the trails on both sides of the mountain range; from Sonora Pass to the Golden Trout Wilderness south of Sequoia and Kings Canyon National Parks. She is well studied in the field of Wildlife and Forestry Conservation and is a member of the Audubon Society, the Nature Conservancy, the Sierra Club, and the Cornell Laboratory of Ornithology. After living most of her life in Fresno, she now resides in Modesto, California, with her husband, Scott.

WHAT'S SO SPECIAL ABOUT UNSPOILED, NATURAL PLACES?

*Beauty   Solitude   Wildness   Freedom   Quiet   Adventure
Serenity   Inspiration   Wonder   Excitement
Relaxation   Challenge*

There's a lot to love about our treasured public lands, and the reasons are different for each of us. Whatever your reasons are, the national **Leave No Trace** education program will help you discover special outdoor places, enjoy them, and preserve them—today and for those who follow. By practicing and passing along these simple principles, you can help protect the special places you love from being loved to death.

THE PRINCIPLES OF **LEAVE NO TRACE**

- Plan ahead and prepare
- Travel and camp on durable surfaces
- Dispose of waste properly
- Leave what you find
- Minimize campfire impacts
- Respect wildlife
- Be considerate of other visitors

Leave No Trace is a national nonprofit organization dedicated to teaching responsible outdoor recreation skills and ethics to everyone who enjoys spending time outdoors.

To learn more or to become a member, please visit us at www.LNT.org or call (800) 332-4100.

Leave No Trace, P.O. Box 997, Boulder, CO 80306